READING POWER

Sports Training

Tennis

Jack Otten

The Rosen Publishing Group's
PowerKids Press™
New York

Published in 2002 by The Rosen Publishing Group, Inc.
29 East 21st Street, New York, NY 10010

First Edition

Book Design: Sam Jordan

Photo Credits: Cover, pp. 4, 6–21 by Maura Boruchow;
p. 5 © Clive Brunskill/AllSport

Thanks to Cardinal Gibbons High School

Otten, Jack.
Tennis / by Jack Otten.
    p. cm. — (Sports training)
Includes bibliographical references (p.) and index.
ISBN 0-8239-5975-9 (lib. bdg.)
1. Tennis—Training—Juvenile literature. [1. Tennis.] I. Title. II.
Series.
GV996.5.O88 2001
796.342—dc21

                                    2001000651

Manufactured in the United States of America

Contents

Introduction

This is Venus Williams. She is a pro tennis player. She plays her best in every game. The young players below want to play like pro players someday.

5

Warming Up

The Nets meet for tennis practice.
The coach helps the team warm up.

The tennis players bend their arms.
They stretch their bodies.

The coach tells a player to do ten
push-ups. Push-ups build strong arms.
Strong arms help tennis players hit
the ball.

Then the coach tells a player
to practice running up to the net.
Running up to the net helps tennis
players learn to stop fast.

Practicing Tennis Swings

Tennis players hit the ball with a racket.

Rackets

Balls

The coach shows this player how to hold the racket for a forehand shot.

The coach shows another player how to make a backhand shot. The player uses two hands to hold the racket. She starts to turn her body away from the ball.

Turns Body

When the ball comes, she swings forward. She follows through and hits the ball.

Swings Forward

This tennis player gets ready to hit a volley. She moves close to the net. She wants to return the ball before it hits the ground.

She hits the ball back over the net into the other player's court.

Practicing Tennis Serves

The coach shows this player how to serve the ball. First, she lifts the racket over her head. Then, she throws the ball into the air.

She brings the racket down quickly.
She follows through to hit the ball.

Practice Games

Two players practice together.
One player serves the ball. The
other player pulls her racket back.

She follows through and hits the ball.

The Nets play a practice game.
They play the way the coach has
taught them.

The players hit the ball well. The coach likes the way the team plays.

Glossary

court (**kort**) a place where tennis is played

practice (**prak**-tihs) to do something again and again to learn to do it well

pro (**proh**) an athlete who gets paid money for playing his or her sport

push-ups (**push**-uhps) exercises done by lying face down and raising the body with your arms

racket (**rak**-iht) an oval wooden or metal frame, with strings and a handle, that is used to hit a ball

serve (**serv**) putting the ball in play

volley (**vahl**-ee) to hit the ball back and forth

warm up (**worm** uhp) to exercise before playing a sport

Resources

Books

The Illustrated Rules of Tennis
by Wanda Tym & Paul Zuehlke
Ideals Children's Books (1995)

Kids' Book of Tennis
by Reggie Vasquez, Jr.
Citadel (1997)

Web Site
http://www.tennis.com

Index

Word Count: 293

Note to Librarians, Teachers, and Parents

If reading is a challenge, Reading Power is a solution! Reading Power is perfect for readers who want high-interest subject matter at an accessible reading level. These fact-filled, photo-illustrated books are designed for readers who want straightforward vocabulary, engaging topics, and a manageable reading experience. With clear picture/text correspondence, leveled Reading Power books put the reader in charge. Now readers have the power to get the information they want and the skills they need in a user-friendly format.